HSC

9/00

Everything
You Need to
Know About

The
Dangers of
Computer
Hacking

Computer hackers are often teenagers just like you.

Everything You Need to Know About

The Dangers of Computer Hacking

John Knittel and Michael Soto

Rosen Publishing Group, Inc./New York

"Step up to red alert."
"Sir, are you absolutely sure? It would mean changing the bulb."
— Red Dwarf

To our parents for our first computers.
To Jennifer for turning off the TV and making us write this book.
To Jazz and Chaos for not sitting on the keyboard when we were trying to finish.

The authors would like to thank the editors of the Jargon File 4.0.0 for creating such a useful reference. The HappyHacker web site also deserves our thanks for supplying us with many hours of entertainment. And finally we would like to give a special thanks to the members of 2600 and AntiOnline for providing us with such interesting reading over the years.

Published in 2000 by The Rosen Publishing Group, Inc.
29 East 21st Street, New York, NY 10010

First Edition

Cataloging-in-Publication Data

Knittel, John, 1973.
    Everything you need to know about the dangers of computer hacking/ John Knittel and Michael Soto.
      p. 23 cm. - (The need to know library)
    Includes bibliographical references and index.
    Summary: This book explains what computer hacking is, who does it, and just how dangerous it can be.
    ISBN: 0-8239-3034-3
    1. Computer crimes—United States.   2. Computer hackers—United States. 3. Internet (Computer network). [1.Computer crimes]
I. Soto, Michael. II. Title. III. Series.
364.16'8—dc21

Contents

	Introduction	6
Chapter One	A History of Hacking	13
Chapter Two	Who Are Hackers?	20
Chapter Three	Knowing the Risks	32
Chapter Four	How Do I Practice Safe Hacking?	47
	Glossary	58
	For Further Reading	61
	Index	63

Introduction

With the rise in popularity of the Internet, the media is filled with more and more reports of computer break-ins and dangerous situations caused by "hackers." The U.S. Department of Defense estimates that their computer systems were attacked 250,000 times during 1995 alone. This means that someone is trying to break into our nation's defense every thirty seconds. It is believed that the total number of break-ins across the entire Internet is ten times as high.

Because of the large number of these attacks and the media's interest in them, law enforcement now considers computer crime a top priority. At the same time, however, computer hacking is still largely misunderstood.

What Is Hacking?

In order to understand what hacking is, you need to know the difference between hacking and cracking.

In the media the term "hacker" is used to describe a person whose only goal is to attack other people's computers and cause them harm. This is not accurate. In reality, hackers are extremely talented people who use their abilities to find innovative ways to change how computers work. They do this by writing new programs and building hardware that no one has thought of before. Hackers use their vast knowledge to better the computer industry.

At the same time, however, there are those who erase other people's files, steal credit card numbers, or vandalize Web pages. Although these people may be called hackers by the media, they are known by people in the computer industry as crackers. They are not highly regarded by those in the computer industry.

So why do the media use the word "hacker" instead of "cracker"? This is mainly for two reasons. When stories are written for newspapers and television, they contain words that everyone is familiar with. Since the general public does not know the term "cracker," the media use the closest thing possible. In this case, the word they use is "hacker." The other main reason is that crackers, wanting to make themselves look better in the public eye, continue to call themselves hackers.

This misuse of terms causes even more confusion in the media when a "good" hacker does something noteworthy. Since the media use the term "hacker" for describing illegal computer break-ins, if a story has to

The Work of Hackers

There are many good hackers out there. Hackers designed and built the Internet. Xerox's Palo Alto Research Center was also made up of hackers, who created many of the early computer and interface designs we are familiar with today.

Many hackers are well known. For example, when Bill Gates started Microsoft, he was a hacker. The software he created made personal computers useful. He designed the first compilers that could be used on a PC. (A compiler is a tool that converts programs into a language the computer can understand.) Gates made it possible for useful software, such as word processors and spreadsheets, to be made and run on your home computer.

Two other hackers, Steve Jobs and Steve Wozniak, started a company called Apple Computer. The computers that Apple built were the first personal computers that anyone could buy and use. When Steve Wozniak built the Apple I computer, he was trying to impress fellow computer hobbyists. If they had not had such an interest in computers, the PCs that everyone loves to use today would probably not exist.

Today Steve Jobs is the head of a company called Pixar, which made the first completely computer generated full-length movie, *Toy Story*.

Steve Wozniak eventually retired from Apple Computer and now teaches fifth- to eighth-grade students how to use computers.

All three of these remarkable individuals were hackers. They did not spend their time breaking into computer systems and causing damage. They simply enjoyed pushing the limits of computer technology.

be written about a good hacker, a term such as "computer expert" is used. For this reason there is rarely a story that mentions a good hacker.

With all of this confusion, people have created new names to clarify the situation. Many good hackers are referred to as white hats, whereas their cracker counterparts are called dark hats. For the purposes of this book, we will generally call them hackers and malicious hackers.

Hacking and Cracking— Crossing the Line

Although there seems to be a clear difference between hacking and cracking, sometimes the line can become blurred.

Hackers can get too curious. In their search for

Steve Jobs is a successful hacker who co-founded Apple Computer.

knowledge, white hats sometimes get themselves into trouble. In 1988 a programmer named Robert Tappan Morris made just such a mistake. He was testing security flaws in two major Internet utilities, "sendmail" and "finger." He decided to write a program that would spread across computers utilizing those flaws, but he misjudged how fast it would spread. His program infected 10 percent of all the computers on the Internet, causing them to slow down and crash. The total damages were estimated at $96 million.

Teens are especially likely to find themselves in the gray area between white hat and dark hat. The Internet is a very complicated place, and if you know how only half of it works, you can make some very big mistakes. Also, it may seem fun and tempting to cause break-ins and mess around with other people's systems. However, rather than being clever and harmless, these maneuvers can land you in jail.

Within the last year, the federal government convicted and prosecuted the first juvenile for computer crime. With these new policies in effect, it is important that the teenagers of today know exactly how much trouble they can get themselves into. This book explains what hacking is, who does it, and just how dangerous it can be.

Famous fictional hackers, the Lone Gunmen from the television show *The X Files* use their computer knowledge to uncover conspiracies.

Chapter One

A History of Hacking

Hacking has a long history—it started even before computers became popular. The earliest form of hacking involved telephones and was called phreaking.

Phreaking began in the early 1970s, when the workings of the phone system were a mystery to everyone except those who ran it. Most people simply took phones for granted. However, a few people tried to figure out just how phones worked. The most famous of these was John Draper. By using a toy whistle from a box of cereal, he was able to take control of AT&T's entire telephone system. He soon became known as "Captain Crunch."

Curiosity eventually led phreakers to be interested in the computers that ran phone systems. Those who changed their focus from telephones to computers later became known as hackers.

Most early computer break-ins came from company employees seeking financial gain or wanting to get revenge in personal disputes. Generally an employee would learn a feature of the computer system and exploit it. For example, in 1971 disgruntled employees at the Honeywell Corporation disabled the Metropolitan Life computer network for a month. Then in 1973, a teller at New York's Dime Savings Bank stole $1 million. Although these incidents are considered computer crime, it was not until the early eighties that crackers, breaking into computer networks that they had no prior relationship with, became widespread.

The release of the movie *War Games* gave many people their first look at hacker society. In this film Matthew Broderick portrays a misunderstood teen who, while trying to play a few new video games, accidentally causes a nuclear scare. The movie introduced thousands of similar teens to a new and potentially dangerous outlet.

Since then, with the widespread availability of computer and network access, the number of teenagers who hack has increased dramatically. A report published by the Computer Emergency Response Team (CERT) showed that from 1989 to 1995, the number of computer attacks increased by over 2,000 percent. With the increase in computer attacks also came an increase in the media's coverage of these events. It wasn't long before hackers gained nationwide notoriety.

Methods Used by Hackers

Just how do these hackers and others like them get in? These are just some of a few simple methods that are used over and over again to gain access to a system. Whereas most are fairly technical, some of them do not even require a computer.

These methods are potentially disastrous for the hacker who uses them. But it is important for everyone to know about them because all computer users are at risk of being exploited.

Dumpster Hopping

Although not very glamorous, one method of finding information is through dumpster hopping. As the name implies, this involves rummaging through a company's trash for documents, memos, or anything that might provide some insight into its computer system. This method also can provide employee names and phone numbers so that hackers can call and ask for passwords.

Social Engineering

How does a hacker call and ask for passwords? No faithful employee would ever give an unauthorized user access to a company's system, would he? Well, by pretending to be a fellow employee or computer administrator, a hacker can make up a story and ask an employee for help: "We're having a little trouble with your computer account. Could you give me your password so that

Malicious hackers might try to fool company employees into giving up passwords or other secret information.

we can log in to correct the problem?" If the story is believable, many people will casually hand over their passwords without thinking twice.

Sometimes hackers do not even have to call. In the past, hackers have fooled people by e-mailing new technical support numbers throughout a company and then simply waiting for the employees to call with questions.

Password Hacking

Whenever a person logs into a computer system, his or her name and password are checked against a password file that is stored on the computer. This file contains acceptable usernames and their passwords in an encrypted (disguised) form. If the name and password entered match a pair in the file, the user is accepted into the system. Otherwise he or she is locked out.

All a hacker has to do to gain entry to a system is find an acceptable match. One way is to repeatedly send usernames and passwords into a computer until a match is found. Although this could be done manually, a hacker will normally use a program that does this automatically. It might take days or months to find a match, but persistence will usually pay off in the long run.

If a hacker already has some access to a computer system, there is another, much more effective method of password hacking. It involves running a program that looks at all of the usernames and passwords that are listed in the password file. It compares the encrypted passwords with a dictionary of common words.

If a password matches a word in the dictionary, the hacker has a new username and password that can be used to log on to the system. For example, if someone in the computer system uses the password "apple," the hacker's program will be able to discover this, and hackers can use that person's account to gain access to the entire system. This is why some computer systems can require that a number be used as part of the password. For example, "Apple7" is a safe password because it does not appear in a dictionary.

Once a hacker has gained access to another person's account, he or she can easily jump to other computers, since most people tend to have the same password on all of the computers they use.

Trojan Horses

Trojan horses are programs that are left behind by hackers after they get onto a computer system. These programs serve many different functions, from erasing important files to allowing the hacker to return anytime he or she wishes.

The greatest difficulty with Trojan horses is that hackers disguise them to look like ordinary programs. Even if you find hackers on your computer system and remove their access, they could easily return using a Trojan horse.

E-mail Snooping

E-mail snooping is the Internet equivalent of listening in on someone else's phone calls. When someone sends an e-mail, the text of the document is simply sent from computer to computer across the Internet until it arrives at the recipient's machine. Using some basic programs, a person can intercept and read these messages. All a hacker has to do is wait for someone to send his or her password to a friend.

War Dialers

Malicious hackers looking for computer systems to break into can use a war dialer. A war dialer is a program that calls a range of phone numbers looking for

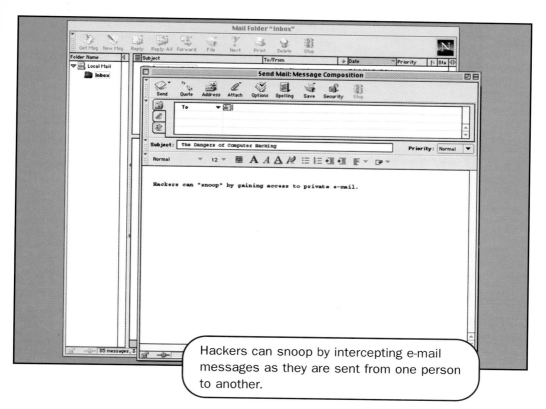

Hackers can snoop by intercepting e-mail messages as they are sent from one person to another.

other computers. When it finds another computer, it notes the number and continues. Malicious hackers can then attempt to break into the computers that are found.

Although many of the methods used to break into computers might seem rather complicated, almost any hacker or cracker can perform them with ease. Mastering the techniques involved, however, takes a great deal of effort. Even more complicated is learning how and why these techniques work.

Chapter Two | Who Are Hackers?

Hackers rarely fit the nerd stereotype of wearing broken glasses and pocket protectors. Usually they are intelligent, individualistic people with highly curious minds. Hackers love to tinker with gadgets and figure out how things work.

Hackers generally have many interests other than computers; they often favor reading, solo sports such as cycling and hiking, and intellectual games such as chess. Their lack of interest in group activities seems to stem from a lack of social interaction. The many hours spent alone in front of computers tends to limit the amount of time spent with other people, and therefore the development of social skills. Socializing via on-line forums and chat rooms can feel much safer than interacting with people face-to-face.

Working alone on a computer may make people favor solo sports instead of group sports.

A Psychological Profile

What specifically leads a person to become a malicious hacker? To answer this we can turn to procedures used by law enforcement officials. When they have a crime to investigate, they like to know what kind of person they are looking for. They create psychological profiles, a group of characteristics shared by many of the people who commit certain crimes, to help them.

Some people have theorized psychological profiles that would help describe describe criminal hackers. At the 1999 RSA Data Security Conference and Expo, Canadian psychologist Marc Rogers gave a talk called "The Psychology of the Hacker." Rogers broke down the general term "hacker" into several subgroups: *newbies, cyberpunks, coders, insiders,* and *cyber terrorists.* Although his is just a theory, it can help you understand what makes malicious hackers do what they do.

- ◆ The two groups that get the attention of the media and law enforcement most often are the newbies and cyberpunks, primarily because they are the ones who frequently get caught. The first group, newbies, are novice computer users with very limited skill. This group tend to get themselves into a lot of trouble because they don't really know what they are doing. When a novice tries to break into a computer system, he or

Newbies, who have limited computer skills, can very easily get into trouble with the law.

she always uses other people's programs to do so. Since the newbie doesn't understand how the program works, the results can be very unpredictable.

Cyberpunks have some programming knowledge and tend to know what they are doing when it comes to breaking computer security. Although they are not experts, they get caught less often than newbies.

The main diffrence between newbies and cyberpunks is their awareness about what they're doing. Newbies have almost no idea how computer systems work and tend to make mistakes when breaking into them.

Cyberpunks, on the other hand, know what they are doing and usually get caught not because they make mistakes but because they brag about their exploits to others.

- The third group, coders, write the programs used by newbies and cyberpunks. Coders have a lot of prestige in the hacker community because they have the most knowledge about the inner workings of computer systems and software. Newbies and cyberpunks aspire to achieve their skill level.

- Seventy to eighty percent of all malicious computer break-ins are committed by insiders. They consist of computer-literate disgruntled employees. Since they already have access to the computer systems, it is very easy for them to cause damage or steal company secrets.

- The most dangerous and least discussed group are professionals, or cyber terrorists. These people hack for profit. They are the most highly skilled group and are almost never mentioned in the media because they rarely get caught. Governments and corporations hire these computer professionals to sabotage computers and steal information from rivals. One of Rogers's main concerns is that almost nothing is known about this

People can become addicted to using computers, spending days at a time in front of them.

group, and because of that, psychological profiles cannot be created for them.

◆ One last group, which is less well defined, is called hacktivists. These are politically motivated malicious hackers who deface Web pages and computer systems to promote their political goals. Unfortunately, it is not clear whether these are actual political groups or cyberpunks covering up their true reasons for breaking into computers in the first place.

Hacker Profiles

An average hacker is a white, middle-class male who is twelve to twenty-eight years old. Even though hackers tend to perform poorly in school, they are very intelligent and curious.

Many hackers have limited social skills; they feel isolated or insecure. As a result they may turn to computers as a way to tune out of reality, especially if their reality is difficult. Teens who are abused or neglected may prefer to explore a world where they feel that they have more power or control. The anonymity of the Internet is very attractive to them—they can choose to be anyone they wish. Hackers may choose impressive on-line names, such as "Destroyer" or "Cyclone," to make up for feelings of low self-worth.

Some teens become so involved in the cyber world that they can sit at a computer for days at a time. Although "computer addictive disorder" has been used as a defense at criminal trials, no medical connection has been made between being addicted to using a computer and committing computer crime.

Three Reasons for Hacking

Within the hacker profile that Marc Rogers developed are three reasons for committing computer crimes. The first is "internal": The entire purpose of the attack is for intellectual motives. Those who hack for this reason do it for the sheer pleasure and benefit of gaining new knowledge.

Another motive for breaking into computer systems is the hope of gaining something. These "external" reasons

Malicious hackers break into computers for many different reasons, including knowledge, money, and even fame. But it is never worth the risk.

can include getting jobs or money for successful computer break-ins. This has been known to happen. Some companies have a policy of hiring hackers as security experts for their computer systems.

"Vicarious" reasoning is the belief that by hacking into a computer system, a person can become famous. Many young people today see stories of hackers and wish that they could have the same kind of recognition. Some hackers have even been praised by their government for breaking into foreign computers.

Opinions about hackers vary widely. They can be seen either as saviors or monsters. Even though the hacking world is a diverse place, everyone in it has one thing in common: They can all get into trouble.

Famous Hackers

There have been many famous hackers. Most of them are well known because they broke the law and got caught. Some have been given long prison terms. Here are examples of two such people:

Justin Tanner Peterson

In 1991 a man named Justin Tanner Peterson, later known as Agent Steal, was arrested for possessing a stolen car. The investigation that followed showed that he was guilty of much more. It turned out that Peterson had been breaking into computer systems. He was indicted for gaining unauthorized access to computers and possessing stolen mail and credit card numbers. Peterson's record was sealed after the FBI and U.S. Attorney's Office asked for him to be released from jail in order to help conduct investigations of other hackers.

He remained under FBI supervision from September of 1991 until October of 1993. During this time Peterson helped the FBI in cases involving two other famous hackers, Kevin Mitnick and Kevin Poulsen. When the case was reopened in 1993, Peterson was faced with up to forty years in jail and a $1.5 million fine. During a meeting with his lawyer and the U.S. attorney, Peterson was asked if he was still committing computer crimes, and he admitted that he was. In fact, he had broken into several federal computers and a credit card information bureau. After realizing his mistake, Peterson asked if he could take a small break. During the break he disappeared. He remained on the run for almost a year, when he was captured only two blocks away from the FBI's west Los Angeles office. In March of 1995, Peterson pleaded guilty to creating an illegal $150,000 wire transfer at Heller Financial. He was given thirty-six months in prison and thirty-six months' supervised detention, and he was fined over $38,000 in restitution.

Kevin Poulsen

The case of Kevin Poulsen, known as Dark Dante, was the first time a hacker was charged with espionage.

Like so many before him, Kevin started out as a phone phreak. At age thirteen, he was already playing with the phone company's internal switching systems. His first arrest was for breaking into the government's Arpanet, which later became the Internet. Later in 1991, he was again arrested for tampering with Pacific Bell's phones.

After years of breaking into government and military computers, Poulsen was offered a job by the defense industry as a security consultant testing Pentagon computer systems. Unfortunately, it appears that protecting government secrets wasn't as interesting to him as stealing them, and Poulsen returned to his former ways. During his employment with the government, Kevin is alleged to have stolen classified military secrets, broken into military computers, stolen records regarding official FBI investigations, and even wiretapped phone calls of Hollywood actresses.

In November of 1989, Kevin Poulsen was indicted for conspiracy, computer fraud, money laundering, and wiretapping. Faced with the possibility of thirty-seven years in jail, Kevin fled. While on the run, Poulsen pulled off one of the most famous stunts in hacker history.

Radio station KISS-FM in Los Angeles had a simple contest. If you were caller number 102 after a certain song was played, you would win a brand-new $50,000 Porsche sports car. While thousands of faithful listeners were calling the station hoping to get lucky, Dark Dante hacked into Pacific Bell and took control of the radio station's phone lines. Only Kevin's phone was able to go through, and all other callers got a busy signal. The prize was his.

After seventeen months the FBI finally caught up with Poulsen. While in custody Kevin attempted to break into FBI computers to erase all of the evidence against him. Espionage charges were added to his indictment when stolen classified documents were found in a locker that Kevin had rented. Poulsen eventually pleaded guilty to computer fraud, money laundering, and obstruction of justice. On April 10, 1995, he was sentenced to fifty-one months in prison and fined over $56,000 in restitution to various radio stations that he had scammed. At the time it was the most severe sentence ever handed down for a computer crime.

Chapter Three

Knowing the Risks

In the past when hackers got into trouble, they would get only probation and a small fine. Now that computers are so important in our daily lives, malicious hackers are seen as a serious threat, and their punishments reflect this.

Unfortunately, maintaining the security of computer systems is often not taken seriously, which makes both deliberate and accidental break-ins more likely. Someone with little computer knowledge can get into trouble very easily.

Companies Are at Risk

With the growth of the Internet, many companies have set up their computers too quickly. In their rush for a presence on the Internet, they fail to adequately prepare

Security in Cyberspace
As E-Commerce Grows

In 1996 a survey was presented at the Senate hearing on "Security in Cyberspace." A small group of security firms were able to account for $800 million in losses worldwide. In that same year, the American Bar Association did a survey of 1,000 companies and discovered that 48 percent of them had lost money because of computer fraud. The damages ranged from $2 million to $10 million. With the dramatic increase in Internet commerce, this can only get worse. According to the Forrester Group in Cambridge, Massachusetts, trade on the Internet will grow from $43 billion in 1998 to $1.3 trillion in 2003. That will be 9.4 percent of all business sales.

the security on those computers. Second, most companies are running too many applications on a single host computer. When a company uses one computer as a Web server, a mail server, and a news server, there are too many things to keep track of. It is simply too difficult to keep secure.

Furthermore, the recent use of the Internet as a commercial venue is a problem. Software vendors are struggling to keep up with new features and as a result are releasing products that are poorly designed, written, and tested. There has been a major increase in commerce activity over the Internet. With all of the

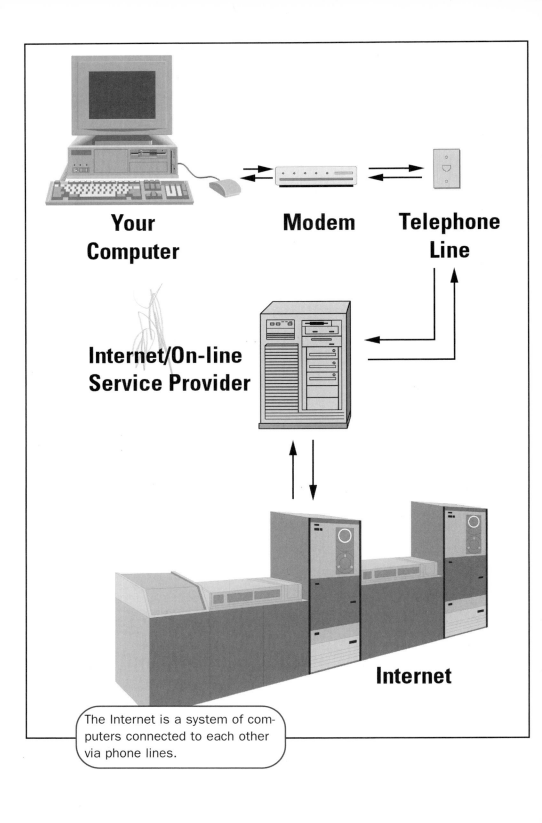

Your Computer

Modem

Telephone Line

Internet/On-line Service Provider

Internet

The Internet is a system of computers connected to each other via phone lines.

security problems on the Web, the financial losses can be staggering.

Once a company's computers are broken into, it can be very difficult to assess the damages. A survey conducted by the Computer Security Institute (CSI) showed that whereas 72 percent of the respondents lost money due to computer break-ins, only 46 percent were able to quantify the amount. Malicious hackers can do a wide variety of things to computer systems. They might only steal information and leave everything as it was before, or they might delete everything. Sometimes the damage is extremely subtle. Companies have huge databases, and if only some of the data is changed, correcting the problem can be quite time consuming.

When malicious hackers break in to steal information, this is called industrial espionage. Many companies and countries hire hackers to steal important company secrets. Not only is this illegal, it can lead to huge financial losses for corporations. In the survey by CSI, companies reported an average loss of over $1.6 million when they were victims of proprietary theft.

E-commerce is probably the area most affected by hackers. Sometimes hackers gain access to computers that have large credit card databases. The credit card numbers can be sold for an enormous amount. A malicious hacker by the name of Carlos Salgado tried to sell a CD-ROM with over 80,000 stolen credit card numbers on it. He was going to sell it for the sum of $260,000.

Unfortunately for him he was trying to sell it to an undercover FBI agent. If Salgado had successfully sold the CD, it could have lead to about $1 billion in credit fraud.

Legal Issues Surrounding Computer Crime

Internet and computer related crimes have been growing faster than the judicial system can keep up with them. Many judges are simply not familiar enough with the material at hand to make accurate decisions. Judges are attending computer and technology seminars trying to figure out how to handle these cases. In 1997 there were only twenty-six convictions under the Computer Fraud and Abuse Act. This does not provide the judges with a great deal of background for their decision making.

Defense attorneys are concerned because they feel that a judge's lack of knowledge could be exploited. Prosecutors can make the crimes appear to be much worse than they actually are. This could lead to very severe sentences.

An additional problem the legal system is facing is the fact that the majority of offenders are juveniles. The federal legal system is not used to dealing with children. Federal crimes generally involve large sums of money, violence, or drugs. This is why juveniles have rarely been accused of committing federal crimes in the past.

"Kids committing computer crimes are generally well

educated, upper middle class, with computers at home and endless time to spend on them," says David E. Green, deputy chief of the U.S. Department of Justice's Computer Crime and Intellectual Property Section. "They are not the kind of people who ordinarily get in trouble with the law." When juveniles are convicted of computer crimes by federal courts, the sentences tend to be lenient. Usually probation is given with the requirement that the youths cannot use a computer for the extent of their probation.

Laws are being adapted to this new kind of crime. For example, in 1994 David M. LaMacchia, a student at MIT, set up an electronic bulletin board for distributing pirated software. The wire fraud statutes at the time did not allow for him to be prosecuted for copyright infringement because he did not profit from his acts. To correct this, the No Electronic Theft Act was passed in late 1997. Now if people give away software illegally, they can be prosecuted even if they don't make any money. In fact, over 200 cases had been prosecuted by the first half of 1998.

In 1996 President Bill Clinton signed the U.S. Economic Espionage Act. The act makes it a federal crime to take, download, or possess trade secret information without consent from the owner. This means that if a hacker breaks into a computer system and looks at any proprietary information that the company might have, he or she is breaking federal law.

The federal government is definitely preparing itself to fight computer crime as the increase in activity is becoming apparent. By March of 1998, the number of case investigations had already doubled the total for the entire year before.

On February 27, 1998, Attorney General Janet Reno unveiled the National Infrastructure Protection Center (NIPC). Made up of several agencies including the FBI, the NIPC will be monitoring investigations into computer-related crimes.

Case Studies

Like Kevin Poulsen and Justin Tanner Peterson, many hackers have gained nationwide attention. The following group of people is comprised of hackers and crackers. They are examples of what can happen when you get caught. Most knew what they were doing; some made honest mistakes. Many of them are just kids; one of them didn't even break into a computer.

Airport Menace

At 9 AM on March 10, 1997, the control tower at Worcester Airport was disabled. For a little over six hours, all vital services, including the main radio trans-mitter, were cut off. Air traffic controllers were forced to use older, more limited backup systems. In addition, telephone lines would not work for the FAA tower or for the airport's fire department. The device that allows airplanes to automatically activate runway lights during landings was useless.

The person who did this was a juvenile computer hacker living in the area. This was the first federal conviction of a juvenile for a computer crime. He was given two years of probation and 250 hours of community service. His computer was confiscated, and he was required to pay restitution to the local telephone company. He was also forbidden from using a computer network or modem directly or indirectly for the length of his probation. This juvenile remains anonymous in accordance with federal law.

Analyzer

In February of 1998, the homes of two teenagers in Cloverdale, California, were raided by FBI agents. The two boys, known on-line as Makaveli and TooShort, had taken part in one of the largest computer attacks the Pentagon had ever seen. They were not formally arrested, but their computers were confiscated. The two youths were eventually placed on probation.

It was soon discovered that their leader was an eighteen-year-old living in Israel named Ehud Tenebaum. Known as Analyzer, he had been teaching the two youths how to get past complex security systems like those used by the government.

The attack included a computer system at NASA, seven U.S. Air Force sites, and four U.S. Navy sites. John

Hamre, the U.S. Deputy of Defense, called it "the most organized and systematic attack the Pentagon has seen to date."

In Israel Tenebaum gained celebrity status after being called "damn good" by Prime Minister Benjamin Netanyahu. A week later he was used in a full-page computer advertisement in Israel's largest newspaper, *Yedioth Ahronoth*. Tenebaum was placed under house arrest in Israel and questioned by local authorities.

Janet Reno stated, "This arrest should send a message to would-be computer hackers all over the world that the United States will treat computer intrusions as serious crimes. We will work around the world and in the depths of cyberspace to investigate and prosecute those who attack computer networks." Tenebaum has been charged in Israel with conspiracy and harming computer systems.

Justin Boucher

Many times the dangers of hacking do not limit themselves to being prosecuted in a court of law. For Justin Boucher, a senior attending Greenfield High School in Milwaukee, Ohio, it resulted in expulsion. In fact, there is no proof that Justin did any hacking at all. At the end of his junior year, Justin wrote for an underground newspaper called *The Last*. Under a pen name, he wrote an article about hacking. The article entitled, "So You Want to Be a Hacker?" outlined methods to break the security of the school's computers.

Ehud Tenebaum, also known as Analyzer, has been charged in Israel with conspiracy and harming computer systems.

When school officials found out that Boucher had written the article, they immediately brought it to the school board's attention. The school board voted unanimously to expel him for fourteen months. Boucher's family, along with the ACLU, sued the school, claiming that it was violating his First Amendment right to free speech. An injunction was issued in September of 1997 to allow Boucher to attend classes while the suit was being resolved. On January 9, however, the Seventh Circuit Court of Appeals stated that the injunction "jeopardized [the school's] authority to control disruptive students" and ruled in favor of the high school.

Kevin Mitnick

Kevin Mitnick is by far the most famous hacker of all time. Descriptions of Kevin range from "cyberhero" to "computer terrorist" depending on whom you ask. Several books have been written about his exploits, and a movie is in the works as well. He has spent more time in jail for computer crime than any other person.

Kevin Mitnick's earliest hacking exploit was breaking into his high school's administrative system. He didn't change any of his grades; he just wanted to see if he could do it. In 1981 Mitnick was arrested for stealing computer manuals from a Pacific Bell switching station. Because he was seventeen, he was given only probation.

In 1982 Mitnick violated his probation. He was caught hacking computers at the University of

Southern California (USC), where he wasn't even enrolled. He served six months at the California Youth Authority's Karl Holton Training School.

While at USC he was reported to have broken into computer systems at NORAD, the North American Air Defense Command in Colorado. It was also believed that Mitnick seized control of phone company systems in New York and California. He was never officially charged for these alleged activities.

Next Mitnick illegally accessed a computer called Dockmaster, the National Security Agency's gateway to the Internet. To gain access he phoned a legitimate user and posed as a technician. By claiming that he was issuing new passwords, Mitnick was able to obtain the user's ID and password.

At age 25 Mitnick was caught hacking into computers at MCI and Digital Equipment. He was accused of causing $4 million worth of damage to computer operations and stealing $1 million worth of software. Mitnick was convicted and given a one-year jail sentence to be served at a minimum-security prison in Lompoc, California. He was ordered not to touch a computer or modem. Upon his release Mitnick was required to spend a year at a residential treatment program, where he took part in a twelve-step program designed to rid him of "computer addiction." Then in 1992, after federal agents came to question him for possible parole violations, he disappeared.

In 1993 California state police issued another warrant for Kevin's arrest. This time he was accused of wiretapping calls from the FBI to the California DMV. He was using supposedly the information to gain illegal entry to the driver's license database.

On Christmas Day, 1994, Mitnick—at the age of thirty—allegedly broke into a computer owned by Tsutomu Shimomura. Shimomura, an expert at computer security, began to track Mitnick. He was arrested in February of 1995. Twenty-five thousand stolen credit card numbers were found on his computer.

This arrest has proved to be the most controversial hacker case of all time. Currently Mitnick is still in jail. In 1996 he pleaded guilty to a federal charge of cellular phone fraud and admitted to violating probation. The next year he was sentenced to two years. He was still awaiting trial for twenty-five counts of computer and wire fraud, possessing unlawful access devices, and intercepting electronic messages.

Because of Mitnick's extremely long incarceration, and suspicion that he was set up, hacker groups began protesting, and the "Free Kevin" movement began in cyberspace. The protests included a legal defense fund that sold bumper stickers and asked for citizens to write to government officials. There is also a Web site devoted to the fund at *http://www.freekevin.com.*

Hacktivists were known to change Web pages in protest for Kevin. The most famous of these activities was in 1997. A group who called themselves PANTS/HAGIS cracked Yahoo, the busiest Web page on the Internet. They changed the site to say that they had planted a virus and that anyone who visited the web site would infect his or her computer. Supposedly the virus was set to go off on Christmas Day if Mitnick was not freed. It turned out that the virus did not exist.

On March 26, 1999, Mitnick accepted a plea agreement that required him to serve a total sentence of sixty-eight months. Formal sentencing was held on August 9, 1999. He was given a 46-month sentence and was ordered to pay $4,125 in restitution. In addition, he is not allowed to touch a computer or cellular phone without written permission from his probation officer.

No Joke

As you can see, computer crime is taken very seriously. Like the case of Justin Boucher, the damage done does not necessarily have to be considered severe to warrant a substantial punishment. When the damage is extensive, as in the case with Kevin Mitnick, the end result can be devastating.

Unfortunately the consequences of your actions cannot always be predicted. Robert Tappan Morris never realized how easily his program could get out of control. If he had been responsible and spent a little more time thinking about the problem, the disaster he caused could have been avoided.

No matter what your age, society will not tolerate reckless behavior. The young man that disabled the airport tower blatantly endangered people's lives. The punishments for this type of action can only get more severe. Understanding the consequences and acting responsibly is the most important factor in becoming a "good" hacker.

Chapter Four

How Do I Practice Safe Hacking?

Computers and software are extremely complicated devices. Learning the intricate details can take many years. If you are seriously interested in becoming a good hacker, you have to be willing to spend time learning about these things. Even if it is only a hobby, you should still have a good understanding of computers.

Learning About Computers

Every day computers are changing. Even after you become an expert, much of your time is spent keeping up with all of the day-to-day changes. True hackers enjoy this very much. To become a computer expert, you must learn a few skills. You don't necessarily have to learn them in this order; but it might make things easier.

One good way to understand how computers and programs work is to use them frequently and explore their features.

First and foremost, are you comfortable using a computer? If you have a computer at home, sit down and play with it. Learn the programs that are installed. One good way to learn is by solving problems. If something is wrong with your computer, try to fix it before you call technical support[1]. You can go onto the Web and find many sites that will explain how to fix technical problems. After a while this will become second nature.

Second, you must be familiar with how the many parts of a computer work. What does the hard drive do? How does a modem work? What is pin number three on an RS232 cable used for?

The next step is programming a computer. You know how to use other people's programs to accomplish a task. Now how do you make a computer do something you want it to? Writing your own programs and understanding the steps involved is probably the most critical measure in becoming a computer expert.

There are many different ways to program a computer. The easiest type of program to write is a script. Scripting languages, such as Perl, JavaScript, and AppleScript, tell other programs to perform certain functions in a specified order. Scripts are very popular to use in Web pages. For example, if you have a Web page, you can use a script to automatically change pictures and

---

1 The authors are not responsible for any harm that you might do to your computer while trying to fix it. Make sure you back up important files before trying something silly.

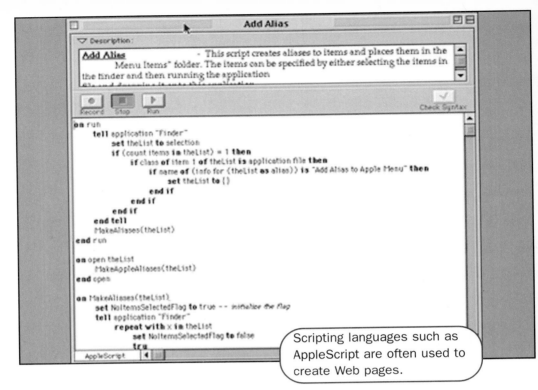

text based on the time of day or to count the number of users that visit your site.

"High-level" programming languages, such as C or Java, allow programmers to create their own applications. To do this, the programmer first writes a list of elaborate instructions that tell a computer how to do something. This code must now be converted from the language that you can understand to the zeros and ones that a computer understands. This is done using a program called a compiler. A compiler creates the finished program that you can run on your computer.

Now that you understand how to make your computer do what you want it to, the next challenge is getting it to talk to other computers. A computer network is a group of machines that are connected so that they can pass

To be an expert computer user, you must know your computer inside and out.

information between each other. The Internet is the world's largest network of computers. Learning the various types of connections and protocols can be very interesting. Writing programs to make them work together may be one of the greatest challenges you will ever face.

Two very important aspects of the computer world that you will have to be familiar with are security and encryption. Security involves writing programs and setting up computers so that only authorized people can use them. If you have a computer or a network and you don't want other people looking at your files, you must set up security. A secure system is one that will keep out unwanted users.

Encryption is a method of making information unreadable to anyone but an intended person. For example, a person can encrypt an e-mail message before

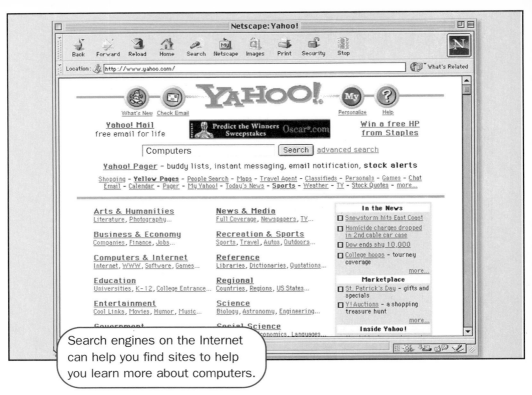

Search engines on the Internet can help you find sites to help you learn more about computers.

sending it across the network. The recipient, knowing the correct password, can then decrypt the message on the other side and read it. If anyone tries to read the message in between, he or she will see only a jumble of letters. This is an excellent way of keeping important information private. To learn cryptography, a person must have a good understanding of mathematics.

Learning About Hacking

Now that it is so easy to access the Internet, learning about safe hacking has never been simpler. If you want to research sites about hacking, go to your favorite search engine. It will have a large listing of security and programming-related Web pages. The Web can provide a wealth of knowledge if you know where to look.

Hackers and Cyber Culture

No one person can learn every aspect of a computer system. It takes hundreds of engineers and programmers just to make them. So the computer community has come up with many ways of sharing information.

Before the Internet, computer enthusiasts communicated via modems and phone lines. They would contact a central computer called a BBS, which stands for "bulletin board system." Messages could be left there for others to read, covering every topic from music to computer programming. Other people could read the messages and reply with their opinions. Hackers could post messages asking others for help or bragging about how they had just fixed a bug in a piece of software. In this way they could easily keep in touch with many of their peers.

Today Internet news groups have virtually replaced bulletin board systems. They are almost exactly the same except that many more people have access to these messages, and the information can be sent automatically to your computer.

On-line chat rooms and Internet Relay Chat (IRC) are also popular forums. These can be thought of as computer party lines. Many people meet to talk about whatever they want to. Unlike a news group, a chat room is a live conversation. When you type something, your friends see it immediately and can type a message back to you. Chat rooms are the perfect meeting place for small groups of hackers discussing the day's events.

Now and then people like to meet in person. Some hacker organizations hold monthly meetings all around the country. The most famous of these meetings is held by a group called 2600. Members gather in malls and other public places to discuss what they are doing and meet other people who are interested in computers and hacking.

Hackers also hold conventions. One of the most popular is called DefCon and is held once a year in Las Vegas. People from all over the world gather together to discuss computer security and other hacker issues. Many lectures are given, and companies set up booths to show off their software. This is a great place for people to exchange information and to be exposed to ideas that may not be covered at their local meetings.

All of these methods are used to communicate information. The information can vary from a new type of encryption that will make the Internet safer to a combination lock that can be broken into in a few minutes. Although a company might not want it known that its locks are unsafe, the hacker community sees it as a benefit to society to make these problems known. They do not promote exploiting this information for illegal purposes.

Many people say that it makes more sense just

to call a company and explain that its product has a security problem. Unfortunately most companies do not correct problems until they have become publicly known. Magazines such as *2600: The Hacker's Quarterly* have brought many potentially disastrous problems into the public eye so that they could be fixed before they were exploited.

One really great Web site is *http:www.AntiOnline.com.* This site is run by security experts who keep track of all the new security breaches and the latest news. AntiOnline also has a search engine that lets you look for whatever problem you might encounter. It even includes a page where it mocks crackers who try to break into its system. It lists where the attack came from and the method used during the attempt.

The International Computer Security Association is an independent corporation that provides security services to its customers. It runs an excellent site at *http:www.icsa.net* where you can browse its library of related articles.

Probably the definitive site for cryptography is *http:www.rsa.com.* Hosted by RSA Data Security, this site provides detailed information on encryption. It also holds contests for cracking various encryption schemes. Winners receive large cash prizes.

Although the Web is a valuable tool, sometimes there

Your local library or bookstore should have a selection of books about computers.

is nothing better than a good book. Your local library or bookstore will offer a number of books on computers; some of them are listed in the For Further Reading section at the end of this book. These computer books cover a large variety of topics, and most of them will state their difficulty level.

What Not to Do

The most important thing to remember when you are learning about computers and hacking is not to do anything illegal. This includes trying to break into a machine when you do not have permission. There some places on the Web that will give you permission—actually asking you to break in. One such example is *http:www.happyhacker.org*. This site offers legal war games in which you can try to hack its systems.

It is important to understand that even if you do not change anything on a computer that you break into, you are still breaking the law. It is also illegal to transmit any computer virus over the Internet. So if you intentionally send someone an e-mail with a virus attached, you could get into trouble.

Staying out of trouble really comes down to common sense. Do you know if what you are doing is wrong? Would you like this done to you? Just remember that an interest in computers can lead either to a high-paying job or to being arrested by the FBI. The line between the two is a fine one—make sure that you stay on the right side.

Glossary

BBS A bulletin board system is a computer that people call using a modem. After calling the computer, a person can send messages to other people and read recent news.

bug A mistake in a computer program.

chat room A place on the Internet where you can talk to other people by typing in messages.

compiler A program that converts programming languages into a form that a computer can understand.

cracker A person who illegally breaks into other people's computers.

cryptography The science of encrypting or deciphering messages.

data Information in a computer.

database An organization of information in a computer that can be easily searched and sorted.

download To transmit a file from another computer to your computer.

e-commerce The buying and selling of goods on the Internet.

e-mail Electronic mail is a message that can be sent across a network.

encryption The method of converting data into a form that cannot be read by others.

hacker A person who uses his or her skills to find new and innovative solutions to computer problems.

ham radio A radio that allows users to communicate with others over long distances.

host Generally, a computer on the Internet that provides services for other computers.

IRC Internet Relay Chat is a popular system for chatting with others on the Internet.

mail server A server that delivers and receives e-mail.

modem A device that allows computers to talk to each other over a phone line. It stands for "modulator/demodulator."

network A system of interconnected computers that can communicate with each other.

news group A forum in which different subjects are discussed on the Internet.

news server A server that delivers and receives news.

password A secret code word that when combined with a username, allows access to a computer.

phreaking The art of breaking into telephone networks illegally.

program A set of instructions for a computer that accomplishes a certain task.

programmer A person who writes programs.

server A computer that provides services, such as e-mail and news, to other computers on a network.

software A generic term for programs that are used on computers.

switching station What telephone companies use to route phone calls.

trojan horse A malicious program that is disguised to look like a seemingly harmless one.

username An identifier that when combined with the correct password, allows access to a computer.

virus A malicious piece of software that inserts itself into other programs on a computer.

war dialer A computer program that uses a modem to call a series of phone numbers looking for other computers.

war game A competition in which hackers can legally attempt to break into a computer.

Web server A server that allows people to see Web pages.

For Further Reading

Books

Cringley, Robert. *Accidental Empires.* New York: HarperCollins, 1993.

Hafner, Katie, and John Markoff. *Cyberpunk.* New York: Simon & Schuster, 1991.

Littman, Jonathan. *The Watchman.* New York: Little, Brown & Co., 1997.

Weigant, Chris. *Careers in Cyberspace.* New York: Rosen Publishing Group, 1997.

Technical Reading

Kernighan, Brian, and Dennis Ritchie. *The C Programming Language.* Toronto, ON: Prentice Hall, 1988.

Schneier, Bruce. *Applied Cryptography.* New York: John Wiley & Sons, 1996.

Web Sites

AntiOnline
http://www.AntiOnline.com

The Computer Emergency Response Team
http://www.cert.org/

Electronic Frontier Foundation
http://www.eff.org/

The Happy Hacker
http://www.happyhacker.org/

International Computer Security Association
http://www.icsa.net/

National Infrastructure Protection Center
http://www.fbi.gov/nipc/nipc.htm

RSA Data Security, Inc.
http://www.RSA.com

Index

A

Apple Computer, 8, 9

B

Boucher, Justin, 42, 45-46
break-ins, 6, 7, 9, 11, 14, 18, 22, 24, 26,
    32, 35, 38, 56

C

coders, 22, 24
compilers, 8, 50
"computer addictive disorder," 26, 44
Computer Emergency Response Team
    (CERT), 14
Computer Fraud and Abuse Act, 36
Computer Security Institute (CSI), 35
credit card fraud, 7, 28, 35-36, 44
cyber terrorists, 22, 24
cyberpunks, 22-24, 25

D

databases, 35, 44
Draper, John, 13
dumpster hopping, 15

E

e-commerce, 33, 35
employees, disgruntled, 14, 24
encryption, 16, 17, 51-52, 54, 55-56
erasing files, 7, 18, 31
espionage, 29, 31, 35

F

FBI, 28-29, 30-31, 35-36, 38, 39, 44,
    57

G

Gates, Bill, 8

H

hacktivists, 25, 45
hardware, 7

I

insiders, 22, 24
International Computer Security
    Association, 55
Internet Relay Chat (IRC), 53
Internet, 6, 8, 11, 18, 26, 30, 32, 33,
    43, 45, 51, 52, 53, 54, 57

J

Jobs, Steve, 8

L

LaMacchia, David M., 37

M

media, 7, 14, 22, 24
Microsoft, 8
Mitnick, Kevin, 29, 42-46
modems, 39, 44, 49
Morris, Robert Tappan, 11, 46

Index

N

National Infrastructure Protection
  Center (NIPC), 38
National Security Agency, 43
newbies, 22-23
No Electronic Theft Act, 38

P

Palo Alto Research Center, 8
password hacking, 16-18
passwords, 15-16, 43, 52
Peterson, Justin Tanner, 28-29, 38
phreaking, 13, 30
Poulsen, Kevin, 29-31, 38
prison sentences/terms, 28, 29, 31, 36,
  37, 44, 45
programs, 7, 11, 17, 18, 22-23, 24, 46, 49,
  50, 51
psychological profiles, 22, 24

R

Rogers, Marc, 22, 24, 26
RSA Data Security, 22, 55

S

Salgado, Carlos, 35-36
scripting languages, 49-50

search engines, 55
security, 23, 28, 30, 32-33, 35, 51, 54-55
software, 8, 33, 37-38, 44, 47, 53, 54

T

technical support, 16, 49
telephone systems, 13, 30, 39, 43
Tenebaum, Ehud, 40
Trojan horses, 18
2600: The Hacker's Quarterly, 55

U

U.S. Department of Defense, 6
U.S. Economic Espionage Act, 38

V

viruses, 45, 57

W

war dialers, 18-19 Web servers, 33
Web pages/Web sites, 7, 25, 45, 49, 52,
  55, 57
wiretapping, 31, 44
Wozniak, Steve, 8, 9

Y

Yahoo, 45

About the Author

Michael Soto is a programmer for a financial corporation in New York City. He is a graduate from The Cooper Union for the Advancement of Science and Art. To the best of his knowledge, he has no other notable accomplishments.

John Knittel is the Manager of Information Systems for a publishing company in New York. He is a graduate from The Cooper Union for the Advancement of Science and Art. His interests are reading and cycling. He has never kissed a girl.

Photo Credits

Cover by Thaddeus Harden. P. 10 © Reuters/Lou DeMatteis/Archive Photos; p. 12 © The Everett Collection; p. 21 by John Bentham; p. 23 © Bachmann/Uniphoto Picture Agency; p. 41 © Reuters/Johonatan Shaul/Archive Photos; all other photos by Thaddeus Harden.

Design and Layout

Annie O'Donnell